EXPLORING WORLD CULTURES

Venezuela

Laura L. Sullivan

Cavendish
Square

New York

Published in 2020 by Cavendish Square Publishing, LLC
243 5th Avenue, Suite 136, New York, NY 10016

Website: cavendishsq.com

This publication represents the opinions and views of the author based on his or her personal experience, knowledge, and
research. The information in this book serves as a general guide only. The author and publisher have used their best efforts
in preparing this book and disclaim liability rising directly or indirectly from the use and application of this book.

All websites were available and accurate when this book was sent to press.

Library of Congress Cataloging-in-Publication Data

Names: Sullivan, Laura L., 1974- author.
Title: Venezuela / Laura L. Sullivan.
Description: First edition. | New York : Cavendish Square, 2020. | Series:
Exploring world cultures | Includes bibliographical references and index. | Audience: Grades 2-5.
Identifiers: LCCN 2018060761 (print) | LCCN 2019001077 (ebook) | ISBN
9781502647177 (ebook) | ISBN 9781502647160 (library bound) | ISBN 9781502647146 (pbk.) |
SBN 9781502647153 (6 pack)
Subjects: LCSH: Venezuela--Juvenile literature.
Classification: LCC F2308.5 (ebook) | LCC F2308.5 .S85 2020 (print) | DDC 987--dc23
LC record available at https://lccn.loc.gov/2018060761

Editorial Director: David McNamara
Editor: Lauren Miller
Copy Editor: Nathan Heidelberger
Associate Art Director: Alan Sliwinski
Designer: Christina Shults
Production Coordinator: Karol Szymczuk
Photo Research: J8 Media

Printed in the United States of America

Contents

Introduction

Venezuela is a fascinating country in South America. It is home to the Andes Mountains, parts of the Amazon rain forest, wide grasslands, and a beautiful coastal region. There are also large and modern cities.

The people of Venezuela are strong. The country has had many political and social problems. Elections are not free or fair. Sometimes there is not enough food to eat. As of 2019, the Venezuelan government is considered a **dictatorship**.

Despite all of this, Venezuelans go to work. The oil industry provides jobs for many people. Venezuelans spend time with their families, and children go to school. They also enjoy sports, music, and festivals during the year. Many tourists also come to Venezuela to see its beaches and historic cities, and to eat delicious foods.

Venezuela is an exciting country to explore!

The Andes Mountains are a beautiful part of Venezuela's landscape.

Geography

Venezuela is located along the northern coast of South America. The Atlantic Ocean and the Caribbean Sea lie to the north. Colombia borders

The capital city of Caracas is found in the mountains.

Venezuela to the west. Brazil lies to the south, and Guyana lies to the east. The country covers 353,841 square miles (916,445 square kilometers).

Caracas is the biggest city and also the capital. About three million people live there.

FACT!

The Rio Negro flows through three countries: Colombia, Venezuela, and Brazil.

Warm and Wet

Venezuela has a tropical climate. Temperatures can average up to 95 degrees Fahrenheit (35 degrees Celsius) in some places. High in the mountains, though, it is much cooler.

The Andes Mountains run through Venezuela. The highest peak is Pico Bolivar. It is 16,332 feet (4,978 meters) tall. There are many

Angel Falls is the world's tallest waterfall!

rivers, including the Rio Negro and the Orinoco. Venezuela is home to the world's tallest waterfall, Angel Falls. It is 3,212 feet (979 meters) tall.

Natives lived in Venezuela for a long time. Then Christopher Columbus arrived in 1498. The Spanish then took over the land. Many Natives died because of diseases brought from Europe.

A portrait of Christopher Columbus

Venezuela declared its independence from Spain on July 5, 1811. The country finally became self-ruling in 1821. Several other South American

FACT!

Simón Bolívar was a Venezuelan leader. He helped free many South American countries from Spanish control.

The Colors of Venezuela

In the Venezuelan flag, yellow symbolizes wealth. Blue stands for the ocean between them and Spain. Red is for the blood shed while fighting for independence.

The Venezuelan flag's colors are important.

countries became independent at that time. Together, they were known as Gran Colombia. During the 1800s, there was a lot of fighting and war.

The discovery of oil in the early 1900s helped Venezuela grow. However, since the 1980s, Venezuela has had many troubles. There was often **corruption** in the government. Venezuela became a dictatorship. Many Venezuelans are poor.

9

Venezuela's government has three parts. The executive part includes the president. The president is elected by a vote to serve a six-year

The assembly meets in the Federal Legislative Palace.

term. The president also chooses a vice president and **cabinet** members.

The legislative part is called the Asamblea Nacional, or National Assembly. It makes the laws. The judicial part includes the Supreme Tribunal of Justice. This court decides if laws are fair.

FACT!

Every citizen over the age of eighteen is allowed to vote.

Giving Natives a Voice

Three seats in the National Assembly are reserved for Native people. These people must be related to the people who lived in Venezuela before the Spanish came.

Money problems, corruption, and violence led to the "Bolivarian Revolution" in 1998. The movement was led by Hugo Chávez. He was president until 2013. Then Nicolás Maduro took over. Many saw him as a dictator. In 2019, Juan Guaidó tried to take over the government. Venezuelans are hoping for a stable government.

Former president Hugo Chávez in 2000

11

The Economy

Once, Venezuela's economy focused on farming. Then, in the early 1900s, oil was found in Venezuela. The country started selling oil to other countries to make money. Today, Venezuela

An oil plant in Puerto La Cruz, Venezuela

has the biggest **oil reserves** in the world.

Oil is Venezuela's biggest industry. The country's economy depends on it. Unfortunately, that means that Venezuela's economy suffers whenever the price of oil drops. Then, when oil

FACT!

The Venezuelan government owns all parts of its oil industry.

12

prices rise, the Venezuelan government often makes the economy worse by overspending. This cycle is still happening in the twenty-first century.

Bolivars show people from Venezuelan history.

Venezuelan money is called the bolivar. As a result of poor money management by the government, the value of the bolivar has gone down. Today, many people can't afford food or other things that they need to live.

Buying Necessities

It is difficult for many people to buy everyday items in Venezuela. One reason is hyperinflation. This means that prices rise a lot in a short amount of time.

The Environment

Venezuela has many plants and animals. Alpacas and huge birds called condors live in the Andes Mountains. The rain forests are home for jaguars, sloths, giant anteaters, and spider monkeys. Alligators, lizards,

Amazon river dolphins are pink!

and snakes live in Venezuela's rivers. Rare Amazon river dolphins also live there. Deer and wild dogs live in the grasslands.

More than 1,500 different orchid species grow in Venezuela.

The World's Largest and Friendliest Rodent

Capybaras live in Venezuela. They are the biggest rodents in the world. They can weigh up to 150 pounds (68 kilograms)!

Capybaras are friendly animals.

Along the northern coast, there are swamps with mangrove trees and birds like ducks, cranes, and herons. Manatees live in the waters there.

Cutting down trees is a big problem in Venezuela. They are chopped down for wood, mining, and oil drilling. The government is working to protect trees and the environment. For example, there are forty-three national parks in Venezuela. In total, 55 percent of the country's land is protected.

Almost thirty-two million people live in Venezuela. Most Venezuelans today have ancestors from the Natives, the Spanish, or the African slaves who were brought to the country.

The Wayuu are the largest Native group in Venezuela.

Venezuelans with European and Native ancestry are called mestizo. Others with Native, European, and African ancestry are called mulatto-mestizo. Over half of the Native

FACT!

The average life expectancy in Venezuela is 76.2 years.

Escaping the Revolution

When Hugo Chávez became president, many Venezuelans worried about the future. Since 1999, more than two million Venezuelans have moved to other countries for safety and better opportunities.

people in Venezuela are from the Wayuu people. Their tribe was never conquered by the Spanish.

Around 85 percent of Venezuelans live in cities. They are often very crowded and dangerous. Many people do not have running water and other necessities. Almost all of the cities in Venezuela are found in the north. Only about 7 percent of people live in the southern part of Venezuela.

17

Lifestyle

Family is very important in Venezuela. Extended families usually live together or nearby. Children often live with their parents until they finish school or get married. Many families are still traditional. They believe men should earn money while women take care of the house and children. However, family roles are slowly becoming more equal.

Family is the center of Venezuelan life.

When couples marry, they usually have two ceremonies—a small civil ceremony and a big church ceremony.

The Venezuelan education system is struggling. About 77 percent of schools don't have running water, electricity, or food services. More than half of students drop out before they graduate.

An elementary school class in Caracas

The students that do finish school often go to college in a different country. They are worried about the high crime and other problems at home. They think they will have better opportunities in another country.

Inequality in Venezuela

According to the law, men and women are equal. In reality, though, men are usually more active in politics and the workforce.

Religion

Most Venezuelans are Christian. Ninety-six percent of Venezuelans are Roman Catholic. Catholics are expected to go to Mass, or service, every Sunday. Some go more often.

Catholics in Venezuela go to Mass at churches like this one.

Two percent of Venezuelans are Protestant. Other religions and those who are not religious make up the last 2 percent. For instance, there are small

FACT!

The Venezuelan constitution guarantees religious freedom.

Most traditional Christian holidays are celebrated in Venezuela, like Christmas and Easter.

communities of Jewish, Muslim, and Buddhist people that live in Venezuela.

Many of the old Native religions have been forgotten. They were replaced when Venezuelans adopted Catholicism. However, the religions of Santeria and Espiritismo still exist. They combine Native, African, and Catholic beliefs. Witchcraft is an important part of these religions. They also share Maria Lionza. She is the saint of peace and nature.

Language

Spanish is the most widely spoken language in Venezuela. It is also the country's official language. Most Venezuelans speak Spanish as their first language. However, many other languages are spoken in the country.

Important signs are written in both Spanish and English.

About forty less common languages are spoken in Venezuela. The most widely spoken

FACT!

Some Native Venezuelan languages are spoken by fewer than twenty people.

New Languages

Immigrants have brought their own languages with them to Venezuela. Some include Italian, Portuguese, Arabic, and German.

Native language is Wayuu. Around 170,000 people speak Wayuu. Other Native languages are only spoken by a few thousand people or less. As a result, many of these languages are dying out.

English is the most widely spoken foreign language. Students have to study English in school. Most kids study English for at least five years. The language is widely used in business. Many people see it as a mark of higher social class to be fluent in English.

Arts and Festivals

The arts in Venezuela are heavily influenced by Spanish culture. For example, religious paintings and Spanish-style architecture are common. Native and African influences are

Devil dancers in a parade for Corpus Christi

also found in Venezuelan art and music.

FACT!

Joropo is Venezuela's national dance. It is similar to a waltz and is danced while holding candles.

Gaita is a popular kind of music. It uses different kinds of drums and stringed instruments. It also uses **maracas**. These are a kind of rattle common in **Latin** music. Today, young musicians are trying to use old, traditional instruments in new music.

Corpus Christi is one of the biggest festivals in Venezuela. It is a religious celebration where people dress as devils with scary masks and parade through the streets. They beat drums and shake maracas. Later, there is a feast and dancing. People also sing songs and read poetry.

Venezuela's National Instrument

The cuatro is the national instrument. It looks like a small guitar.

Fun and Play

Venezuela's most popular sport is baseball. It became popular when workers from the United States moved to Venezuela for oil jobs. Now, people of all ages love watching it and playing for fun.

José Altuve is a baseball star from Venezuela.

Basketball and volleyball are also favorites. Soccer is becoming more popular in Venezuela. The Venezuelan national team has been improving over the past couple years. Golf used to be popular in Venezuela. However, when

FACT!

Venezuela has won fifteen Olympic medals. Six of them were for boxing.

Colorful Uniforms

The national soccer team is nicknamed Vino Tinto (VEE-no TEEN-toh), or "wine colored," for their burgundy uniforms.

Chávez became president he closed many golf courses. He believed they were for the rich. Today, golf is more accepted as a sport for everyone. Jhonattan Vegas is Venezuela's most famous professional golfer.

Hikers from around the world come to climb Mount Roraima.

Venezuela's many national parks are great places to go rafting, kayaking, hiking, and mountain climbing. People also enjoy swimming and fishing at the beaches along the northern coast.

Food

Like most aspects of Venezuelan life, the food is a mix of Native, Spanish, and African cultures.

Quesillo is the Venezuelan version of flan.

There are big cattle ranches in Venezuela, so beef is a common ingredient. Meat is often grilled over a fire. Fish like snapper and mahi-mahi are popular near the coast. Other traditional ingredients include rice, yams, corn, and beans.

FACT!

Quesillo (kay-SEE-oh) is a popular dessert made of caramel custard.

Putting Food on the Table

In 2018, food shortages were a serious problem. Some people had to wait hours in line to get groceries.

Breakfast might include fruit-filled pastries or scrambled eggs with tomatoes and onions. Arepas (ah-RAY-pahs), small loaves of bread made from corn flour, are stuffed with meat, rice, beans, and more. They are eaten for meals and snacks.

Pabellón criollo (pah-bay-ON cree-OH-yoh) is Venezuela's national dish. It is shredded beef served with rice and black beans. It is often served with fried **plantains**, or with a fried egg on top.

Pabellón criollo is tasty and filling!

Glossary

cabinet   A group of people who advise the president of a country.

corruption   Dishonest or illegal behavior by someone in a powerful position.

dictatorship   A government in which the leader has total control over the country.

Latin   Relating to the countries of Central and South America.

maracas   A hollow musical instrument that rattles.

Natives   The first people to live in a certain area.

oil reserves   Oil that hasn't been removed from the ground yet.

plantains   A starchy, banana-like fruit that is eaten cooked.

Find Out More

Books

Borngraber, Elizabeth. *The People and Culture of Venezuela.* New York: PowerKids Press, 2018.

Tustison, Matt. *Jose Altuve: Baseball Star.* Mendota Heights, MN: Focus Readers, 2018.

Website

Ducksters: Venezuela

https://www.ducksters.com/geography/country.php?country=Venezuela

Video

Kids Around The World—The Music of Venezuela

https://www.youtube.com/watch?v=ZMj6S5MM0E8

This video teaches kids about traditional Venezuelan music.

31

Index

About the Author

Laura L. Sullivan is the author of more than forty fiction and nonfiction books for children, including the fantasies *Under the Green Hill* and *Guardian of the Green Hill*. She lives in Florida where she likes to bike, hike, kayak, hunt fossils, and practice Brazilian jiujitsu.